D0926455

Doña Felisa Rincón de Gautier
Mayor of San Juan

Written by Magali García-Ramis
Illustrated by Pauline Howard

MODERN CURRICULUM PRESS

Program Reviewers

Leslie Anderson-Olrich, Teacher
   Martin Luther King, Jr. School
   Oakland, California

Jimmie Rabalais, Elementary Supervisor
   Curriculum Center
   Rapides Parish School System
   Alexandria, Louisiana

Rachel Sing, Doctoral Candidate
   Harvard University
   School of Education
   Cambridge, Massachusetts

Eloise Andrade Laliberty,
   Bilingual Teacher
   St. Vrain Valley School District
   Longmont, Colorado

Evangeline Nicholas, Ed. D.
   Author and Educational Consultant
   Chicago, Illinois

Executive Editor: Janet Rosenthal
Project Editors: Elizabeth Wojnar
                Mark Shelley

MODERN CURRICULUM PRESS

An imprint of Paramount Supplemental Education
250 James Street
Morristown, New Jersey 07960

ISBN 0-8136-6077-7   (Reinforced Binding)   0-8136-5736-9 (Paperback)
Library of Congress Catalog Card Number: 94-077302

10 9 8 7 6 5 4 3 2 1   **SP**   99 98 97 96 95 94

Dear Reader,

This is the story of Doña Felisa Rincón de Gautier. She was the first woman mayor of the city of San Juan, Puerto Rico.

From the time Felisa was a small girl, she knew she wanted to help people. As she grew up, Felisa learned how important it was for everyone to help make our cities safe and clean places to live.

Felisa has always taught people to work together for the good of all. As you read about Felisa's life, think about what you can do to help others.

Your friend,

Magali Garcia Ramis

A baby sat smiling in the warm sun. She
held a colorful flower tightly in her
hands. The baby was Felisa Rincón and
she lived in Ceiba, Puerto Rico. Puerto
Rico is an island Southwest of the state
of Florida.

Felisa's father, Enrique Rincón, was a
lawyer and a poet. Her mother, Rita
Rincón, was a teacher.

As a young girl, Felisa loved
to read. She was a curious
child who always wanted
to learn about new things. Felisa
also liked to sew and dance.

3

In 1908, when Felisa was eleven years old, her mother died. Felisa told her father, "Don't worry Papa, I know how to take care of little children. I will help you." Felisa had seven younger brothers and sisters.

Felisa worked hard. After school she
cooked and sewed for her family. At
night, her father's friends would often
visit. They talked about the people of
San Juan. Many people needed good
homes and schools. Felisa listened
and wondered, "Who can help these
people?"

When Felisa was in high school, the family moved to a farm. Felisa helped to grow pineapples, plantains, and flowers. After her third year in high school, Felisa stopped going to school. She was needed at home.

Felisa was sad when she saw how many farm workers lived. Their homes were small huts without electricity or water. Again, Felisa wondered, "Who can help these people?"

Felisa took care of her father and her younger brothers and sisters for many years. In 1932, Felisa was thirty-five years old. Puerto Rican women had just won the right to vote. Felisa wanted to vote, too. When hundreds of women went to sign up, Felisa was one of the first in line.

Shortly after signing up to vote, Felisa was looking for new experiences. She traveled by boat from Puerto Rico to New York. Felisa's sister, Fini, and her cousin, Maria, went too.

In New York, they sewed clothes in a women's clothing store. Felisa was doing very well. But she missed her family and friends. After only a few months, Felisa decided to return to Puerto Rico.

12

When Felisa returned home, she opened a dress shop with Fini. They opened the shop in San Juan, the capital city of Puerto Rico. Sometimes Felisa gave away cloth and dresses to families who needed clothing but did not have much money.

As time passed, many people in San Juan got to know Felisa. They thought that she should run for a government office. The people of San Juan wanted Felisa to help them solve some of the problems in their city.

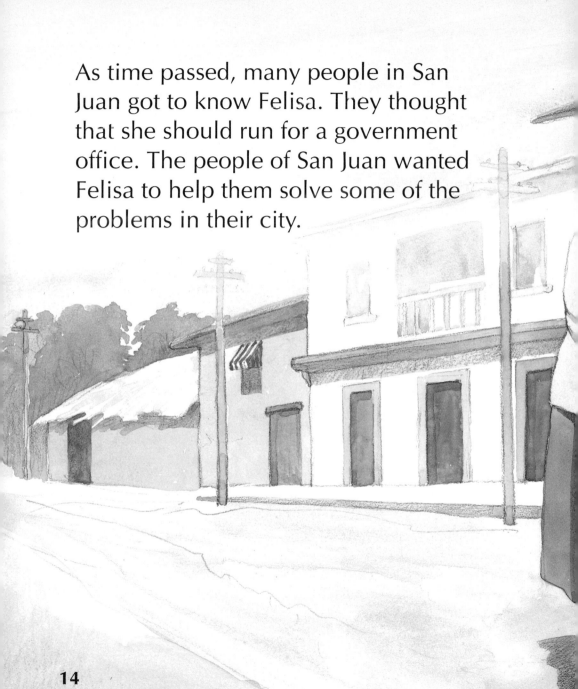

15

When Felisa was forty-three years old,
she married Jenaro Gautier. Jenaro was a
lawyer. Felisa and Jenaro worked
together. They walked all over San Juan
and saw what needed to be done to
change the city. Everyone admired Felisa
because she worked so hard.

In 1946, Felisa found a way to do the
most good. She became the first
woman mayor of San Juan, Puerto
Rico. "Now I know who can help the
people of San Juan. I can!" Felisa said.

19

Felisa quickly went to work as the mayor of San Juan. She opened medical offices, fixed houses, and collected food for hungry families. Felisa also started day-care centers and schools for the children of San Juan whose families had little money. Thanks to Felisa's work, many girls and boys went to high school and college.

21

To make the city safe and clean, Felisa asked the city council to buy new fire trucks and garbage trucks. She proudly watched as firefighters and garbage collectors rode their new trucks in city parades. Often, children rode in the trucks during the parades, too.

Soon people started to call Felisa by the nickname Doña Fela. Doña is a title of respect. The people of San Juan called her this because she was a special person to them.

24

Felisa is very proud of San Juan, Puerto Rico and its people. As mayor of the city for over twenty years, she helped to make it a better place to live.

If you ever visit San Juan, you can go to the Museum of Doña Fela. In this museum they have photos of much of the work Felisa has done for the city of San Juan.

Glossary

admire (ad′ mīr) to respect someone very much

curious (kyoor′ē əs) to want to learn or know

electricity (ē lek′tris′i tē) power that makes things like lamps, heaters, and televisions work

lawyer (lô′ yər) one trained in the law, who helps others in problems with the law

plantain (plan′tin) a type of banana that is eaten as a vegetable after it is cooked

About the Author

Magali García-Ramis is a writer and journalism teacher at the University of Puerto Rico. She was born and raised in San Juan, Puerto Rico. Ms. García-Ramis believes it is very important for children of all cultural backgrounds to know the history and traditions of their people so that they can be proud of who they are when they grow up. This book is dedicated to all children who are learning to read, especially her nieces, Andrea and Adriana.

About the Illustrator

Pauline Howard is a native Texan of Spanish and Polish ancestry. Since graduating from the University of Houston with a degree in art, Ms. Howard has become well known for her paintings of children, ballet, and horses. In *Doña Felisa,* she used pencil, colored pencil, and watercolor in a representational style.